Practical
Pre-School Books

Match your theme to the EYFS

Planning for Learning through Celebrations and Festivals

by Rachel Sparks Linfield

Contents

Published by Practical Pre-School Books, A Division of MA Education Ltd,
St Jude's Church, Dulwich Road, Herne Hill, London, SE24 0PB Tel: 020 7738 5454

www.practicalpreschoolbooks.com

© MA Education Ltd 2020.

Front cover image taken by Lucie Carlier. Back cover images taken by: Rachel Linfield (left) and Niall Waller (right).
Photo on page 19 taken by Niall Waller. 'Party words' on page 18 by Rachel Gillham. © MA Education Ltd.

Planning for Learning through Celebrations and Festivals ISBN: 978-1-912611-27-0

Making plans

Child-friendly planning

The purpose of planning is to make sure that all children enjoy a broad and balanced experience of learning. Planning should be flexible, useful and child-friendly. It should reflect opportunities available both indoors and outside. Plans form part of a planning cycle in which practitioners make observations, assess and plan.

Children benefit from reflective planning that takes into account the children's current interests and abilities and also allows them to take the next steps in their learning. Plans should make provision for activity that promotes learning and a desire to imagine, observe, communicate, experiment, investigate and create.

Plans should include a variety of types of activity. Some will be adult-initiated or adult-led, that focus on key skills or concepts. These should be balanced with opportunities for child-initiated activity where the children take a key role in the planning. In addition there is a need to plan for the on-going continuous provision areas such as construction, sand and water, malleable materials, small world, listening area, role-play and mark-making. Thought also needs to be given to the enhanced provision whereby an extra resource

or change may enable further exploration, development and learning.

The outdoor environment provides valuable opportunities for children's learning. It is vital that plans value the use of outdoor space.

The UK Frameworks

Within the UK a number of frameworks exist to outline the provision that children should be entitled to receive. Whilst a variety of terms and labels are used to describe the Areas of Learning there are key principles which are common to each document. For example they advocate that practitioners' planning should be personal based on observations and knowledge of the specific children within a setting. They acknowledge that young children learn best when there is scope for child-initiated activity. In addition it is accepted that young children's learning is holistic and although within the documents Areas of Learning are presented separately in reality children's activities and explorations cross over and combine with different subject areas. Thus the Areas of Learning are perhaps of most use for planning, assessment and recording to ensure that key areas are not overlooked.

Focused area plans

The plans you make for each day will outline areas of continuous provision and focused, adult-led activities. Plans for focused-area activities need to include aspects such as:

● resources needed
● the way in which you might introduce activities
● individual needs
● the organisation of adult help
● size of the group
● timing
● safety
● key vocabulary.

Identify the learning and the Early Learning Goals that each activity is intended to promote. Make a note of any assessments or observations that you are likely to carry out. After carrying out the activities, make notes on your plans to say what was particularly successful, or any changes you would make another time.

Making plans

A final note

Planning should be seen as flexible. Not all groups meet every day, and not all children attend every day. Any part of the plan can be used independently, stretched over a longer period or condensed to meet the needs of any group. You will almost certainly adapt the activities as children respond to them in different ways and bring their own ideas, interests and enthusiasms. The important thing is to ensure that the children are provided with a varied and enjoyable curriculum that meets their individual developing needs.

Using the book

Read the section which outlines links to the Early Learning Goals (pages 4 - 6) and explains the rationale for focusing on 'Celebrations and Festivals'.

The chart on page 7 gives an example format for weekly planning. It provides opportunity to plan for the on-going continuous provision, as well as more focused activities.

Use pages 8 to 19 to select from a wide range of themed, focused activities that recognise the importance of involving children in practical activities and giving them opportunities to follow their own interests. For each 'Celebrations and Festivals' theme, two activities are described in detail as examples to help you in your planning and preparation. Key vocabulary, questions and learning opportunities are identified. Use the activities as a basis to:

●   extend current and emerging interests and capabilities
●   engage in sustained conversations
●   stimulate new interests and skills.

Find out on page 20 how the 'Celebrations and Festivals' activities can be brought together within a special 'Celebration Party'.

Use page 21 for ideas of resources to collect or prepare. Remember that the books listed are only suggestions. It is likely that you will already have within your setting a variety of other books that will be equally useful.

The activity overview chart on page 23 can be used either at the planning stage or after each theme has been completed. It will help you to see at a glance which aspects of children's development are being addressed and alert you to the areas which may need greater input in the future.

As children take part in the activities, their learning will progress. 'Collecting evidence' on page 22 explains how you might monitor each child's achievements.

There is additional material to support the working partnership of families and children in the form of a reproducible Family Page found inside the back cover.

It is important to appreciate that the ideas presented in this book will only be a part of your planning. Many activities that will be taking place as routine in your group may not be mentioned. For example, it is assumed that sand, dough, water, puzzles, role-play, floor toys, technology and large-scale apparatus are part of the ongoing early years experience. Role-play areas, stories, rhymes, singing, and group discussion times are similarly assumed to be happening in each week although they may not be a focus for described activities.

Health and Safety

As many celebrations and festivals incorporate food, some activities within this book involve food. Always ensure that before these take place risk assessments have been carried out and knowledge of children's food allergies and intolerances have been considered, along with families' religious and diet preferences.

Using the 'Early Learning Goals'

Page 2 describes the principles that are common to each of the United Kingdom curriculum frameworks for the Early Years. It is vital that, when planning for children within a setting, practitioners are familiar with the relevant framework's content and organisation for areas of learning. Regardless however, of whether a child attends a setting in England, Northern Ireland, Scotland or Wales they have a right to provision for all areas of learning. The children should experience activities which encourage them to develop their communication and language; personal, social, emotional, physical, mathematical and creative skills. They should have opportunities within literacy and be encouraged to understand and explore their world.

Within the *Statutory Framework for the Early Years Foundation Stage* (2014), Communication and Language; Physical Development and Personal, Social and Emotional Development are described as Prime Areas of Learning that are 'particularly crucial for igniting children's curiosity and enthusiasm for learning, and for building their capacity to learn, form relationships and thrive' (page 7, DfE 2014). The Specific Areas of Learning are Literacy, Mathematics, Understanding the World and Expressive Arts and Design.

For each Area of Learning the Early Learning Goals (ELGs) describe what children are expected to be able to do by the time they enter Year 1. These goals, detailed on pages 4 to 6, have been used throughout this book to show how activities relating to 'Celebrations and Festivals' could link to these expectations. For example, for Personal, Social and Emotional Development, one aim relates to the development of children's 'self-confidence and self-awareness'. Activities suggested which provide the opportunity for children to do this have the reference PSE1. This will enable you to see which parts of the Early Learning Goals are covered for a given theme and to plan for areas to be revisited and developed.

In addition, an activity may be carried out to develop a range of different Early Learning Goals. For example, making models of celebration cakes from boxes will offer a variety of learning opportunities. Children will explore and use materials for Expressive Arts and Design. In addition, they will have the opportunity to develop their awareness of shape and size as they remake cereal packets inside out to give clear surfaces, and combine different box sizes to make a 'cake'. Working in groups children will make relationships and develop in confidence as they make choices of resources and give reasons for their selections. Thus, whilst adult-focused activities may have clearly defined goals at the planning stage, it must be remembered that as children take on ideas and initiate their own learning and activities, goals may change.

The Prime Areas of Learning

Communication and Language

Listening and attention: children listen attentively in a range of situations. They listen to stories, accurately anticipating key events and respond to what they hear with relevant comments, questions or actions. They give their attention to what others say and respond appropriately, while engaged in another activity. (CL1)

Understanding: children follow instructions involving several ideas or actions. They answer 'how' and 'why' questions about their experiences and in response to stories or events. (CL2)

Speaking: children express themselves effectively, showing awareness of listeners' needs. They use past, present and future forms accurately when talking about events that have happened or are to happen in the future. They develop their own narratives and explanations by connecting ideas or events. (CL3)

'Celebrations and Festivals' provide many opportunities for children to enjoy listening, understanding and speaking. There are a wide range of books featuring celebrations and festivals and these can be used to stimulate interest in the chosen themes, encouraging children to listen and to talk. Considering both what we celebrate and how we celebrate, lets children explore picture, story and fact books. When looking at pictures of celebrations, exploring celebrations cards and decorations, and collaborating to plan the 'Celebrations Party' children will have the opportunity to listen, to speak and to ask questions. When making floating, paper flowers, children will follow instructions. Talking about personal experiences of celebrations, will encourage children to express themselves and to show awareness of listeners' needs.

Physical Development

Moving and handling: children show good control and co-ordination in large and small movements. They move confidently in a range of ways, safely negotiating space. They handle equipment and tools effectively, including pencils for writing. (PD1)

Health and self-care: children know the importance for good health of physical exercise, and a healthy diet, and talk about ways to keep healthy and safe. They manage their own basic hygiene and personal needs successfully, including dressing and going to the toilet independently. (PD2)

Physical development is an important area where children need opportunities to understand and value physical skills and the importance of healthy exercise. A whole range of activities are described for 'Celebrations and Festivals' to enable children to develop skills and confidence, and to enjoy movement and handling tools and equipment. When children dance to music from around the world, become fireworks outside using streamers and ribbons and role-play camping at a music festival they can develop and demonstrate control and co-ordination. Making divas from clay, cutting used cards and using chopsticks will allow children to use small equipment and promote the development of fine motor skills. In addition, any of the described literacy activities, where children write, will also contribute to the development of 'handling' skills. Areas such as basic hygiene and going to the toilet independently will be part of on-going, daily activity.

Personal, Social and Emotional Development

Self-confidence and self-awareness: children are confident to try new activities, and say why they like some activities more than others. They are confident to speak in a familiar group, will talk about their ideas, and will choose the resources they need for their chosen activities. They say when they do or don't need help. (PSE1)

Managing feelings and behaviour: children talk about how they and others show feelings, talk about their own and others' behaviour, and its consequences, and know that some behaviour is unacceptable. They work as part of a group or class, and understand and follow the rules. They adjust their behaviour to different situations, and take changes of routine in their stride. (PSE2)

Making relationships: children play co-operatively, taking turns with others. They take account of one another's ideas about how to organise their activity. They show sensitivity to others' needs and feelings, and form positive relationships with adults and other children. (PSE3)

'Celebrations and Festivals' is an ideal context for both child-initiated and adult-led activities which enable children to work towards goals in the Personal, Social and Emotional Development Area of Learning. Activities focusing on the celebrations and festivals that take part within children's own families encourage children to speak, to share ideas and to show sensitivity to others' needs and feelings. They provide opportunities to explore their own and other cultures and for staff to model and encourage a sense of respect. Group discussion and small group activities promote co-operation

and build relationships. Many of the areas described within the ELGs for Personal, Social and Emotional Development though, will be covered on an almost incidental basis. Any activity that involves making choices, or showing initiative, will promote self-confidence and self-awareness.

The Specific Areas of Learning
Literacy

Reading: children read and understand simple sentences. They use phonic knowledge to decode regular words and read them aloud accurately. They also read some common irregular words. They demonstrate understanding when talking with others about what they have read. (L1)

Writing: children use their phonic knowledge to write words in ways which match their spoken sounds. They also write some irregular common words. They write simple sentences which can be read by themselves and others. Some words are spelt correctly and others are phonetically plausible. (L2)

Activities for 'Celebrations and Festivals', based on picture books and stories, will provide opportunities for the children to read using both their phonic knowledge and memories of common, irregular words. Discussions of the stories will help children to understand and to develop their vocabularies. Making name acrostics for the 'celebrating diversity' theme; collecting words for celebrations and festivals and exploring words in celebration cards, will encourage children to experiment with letters and sounds. Activities such as writing posters for a music festival, celebration certificates and New Year resolutions, and role-play in a music festival ticket office will encourage children to enjoy the early stages of writing.

Planning
for
Learning
through
**Celebrations
and Festivals**

5

Mathematics

Numbers: children count reliably with numbers from 1 to 20, place them in order and say which number is one more or one less than a given number. Using quantities and objects, they add and subtract two single-digit numbers and count on or back to find the answer. They solve problems, including doubling, halving and sharing. (M1)

Shape, space and measures: children use everyday language to talk about size, weight, capacity, position, distance, time and money to compare quantities and objects and to solve problems. They recognise, create and describe patterns. They explore characteristics of everyday objects and shapes and use mathematical language to describe them. (M2)

Activities for 'Celebrations and Festivals' provide many opportunities for children to count, to measure and to explore pattern, shape and space. Sorting children's birthday months; looking at the number of layers within tiered wedding cakes; counting with the 'Crown a cake with candles' number rhyme; exploring amounts in recipes for special, festival foods and looking at the number of coins in red Chinese New Year money packets will encourage children to count and to use numbers in everyday life. Creating Chinese New Year dragons with cardboard tubes, and making wrapping paper by printing with solid shapes, helps to develop children's recognition and knowledge of the properties of shapes. Making panpipes with straws provides further opportunity to count and to use size vocabulary whilst comparing lengths.

Understanding the World

People and communities: children talk about past and present events in their own lives and in the lives of family members. They know that other children don't always enjoy the same things, and are sensitive to this. They know about similarities and differences between themselves and others, and among families, communities and traditions. (UW1)

The world: children know about similarities and differences in relation to places, objects, materials and living things. They talk about the features of their own immediate environment and how environments might vary from one another. They make observations of animals and plants and explain why some things occur, and talk about changes. (UW2)

Technology: children recognise that a range of technology is used in places such as homes and schools. They select and use technology for particular purposes. (UW3)

Through involvement in activities based around 'Celebrations and Festivals' children have great opportunity to develop a real understanding of the world around them, to explore and to relate what they discover to both previously held ideas and future learning. The themes encourage children to share their experiences of the celebrations and festivals that they enjoy with their own families whilst at the same time gain awareness of the diversity within their peers, their setting and the wider community. Activities which involve the handling of materials such as making noisy shakers for the Chinese New Year; tasting celebratory foods; doing handprints for henna patterns and making Christingles encourage children to investigate and to ask questions. Use of technology to research aspects of festivals and celebrations such as decorations, clothes, fireworks and food, and for recording events, will help the children to recognise that a range of technology can be useful. Technology will also feature in role-play as well as being part of the on-going, daily provision.

Expressive Arts and Design

Exploring and using media and materials: children sing songs, make music and dance, and experiment with ways of changing them. They safely use and explore a variety of materials, tools and techniques, experimenting with colour, design, texture, form and function. (EAD1)

Being imaginative: children use what they have learnt about media and materials in original ways, thinking about uses and purposes. They represent their own ideas, thoughts and feelings through design and technology, art, music, dance, role-play and stories. (EAD2)

Whilst involved in activities for 'Celebrations and Festivals', children will experience working with a variety of materials, tools and techniques as they make collages of faces; create Rangoli patterns; make necklaces from paper plate rims and shiny decorations. When changing words for songs, experimenting with percussion and playing in the role-play tent for a music festival, children have the chance to be imaginative. Throughout all the activities children should be encouraged to talk about what they see and feel as they communicate their ideas in painting, model making, music and role-play.

Note

The Early Learning Goals raise awareness of key aspects within any child's development for each Area of Learning. It is important to remember that these goals are reached through a combination of adult and child-initiated activity within Early Years settings and, also, a child's home life. Thus, it is vital that goals are shared by practitioners and parents, and children are given every opportunity to develop throughout their Early Years Foundation Stage at home and within a setting.

Example chart to aid planning in the EYFS

Week beginning:	Monday	Tuesday	Wednesday	Thursday	Friday
FOCUSED ACTIVITIES					
Focus Activity 1:					
Focus Activity 2:					
Stories and rhymes					
CONTINUOUS PROVISION (Indoor)					
Collage					
Construction (large)					
Construction (small)					
Imaginative play					
Listening					
Malleable materials					
Mark making					
Painting					
Role-play					
Sand (damp)					
Sand (dry)					
Technology					
Water					
CONTINUOUS PROVISION (Outdoor)					
Construction					
Creative play					
Exploratory play					
Gross motor					
ENHANCED PROVISION (Indoor)					
ENHANCED PROVISION (Outdoor)					

Theme 1: What we celebrate

Communication and Language

- Introduce the words 'celebrate' and 'celebration'. Talk about things the children and their families enjoy celebrating. Include both large scale events and family ones. Has anyone been to a wedding? Did anyone go to a Bonfire Night display? What happened? (CL3)
- Look at photos of families celebrating events such as Diwali, the Chinese New Year, Eid, and Christmas. How can we tell people are celebrating? Encourage children to notice people's happy faces and to ask questions about the celebrations. (CL2)
- Share stories about celebrations. Talk about the key features that make an event a celebration. (CL1)

Physical Development

- Talk about favourite party games. Enjoy playing traditional party games that involve movement, both inside and in the outdoor space. (PD1)
- Dancing is a feature of many celebrations and festivals. Play music and encourage the children to enjoy moving, in time, to the music. Investigate Youtube for ceildh or barn dance music. Play this type of music and encourage children to dance with a partner. (PD1)
- Explain that eggs are often given at Easter to celebrate new life. In some areas of the world games are played with eggs to celebrate Easter. Hold an egg event where all the games are based on 'eggs' (see activity opposite). (PD1)

Personal, Social and Emotional Development

- Encourage children to talk about feelings they have when they celebrate something. Also talk about feelings after a celebration has just finished! (PSE2)
- Talk about events that happen to celebrate birthdays such as parties, birthday cakes and giving cards and presents. Set up a role-play area for children to plan and hold celebrations for soft toys, dolls or peers. (PSE3)
- Play a game where children pass an empty box around the circle, to music. When the music stops the child holding the box says "In my celebrations box there is/ are ...") and finishes the sentence with a word for an object or action to do with celebrations. This may also be played as an 'add on' game where each time the music stops the child is encouraged to repeat what has been said previously, before adding their own idea. PSE3)

Literacy

- Either show the children certificates that adults in the setting received as a child to celebrate an event such as swimming 10 metres or making a Beaver/Rainbow promise or, if children have received certificates, invite them to 'show and tell'. Make certificates for events in the setting that children feel should be celebrated. Help the children to write their name, date and reason for the certificate. (L2)
- Begin to collect words for celebrations and festivals. Write the words on pieces of card and place them in shoe boxes covered in celebratory wrapping paper. In one box put the names of celebrations (e.g. Bonfire Night, Halloween, Easter, Eid ...). In a second box, put words to describe the events (e.g. happy, loud, scary, loving ...). In a final box put the names of objects and happenings for the celebrations (e.g. crackers, decorations, red packets, divas ...). In small groups enjoy sorting the words and using them to build sentences. Invite children to suggest new words to go in the boxes. (L1)

Mathematics

- Talk about the red packets that are given and received to celebrate the Chinese New Year. Enjoy counting activities using red envelopes (see activity opposite). (M1)
- Make a 'birthday train display' to show children's birthday months (see display ideas). Use the display for comparing amounts. How many children have birthdays in June? Is there the same number in another month? Which month has the fewest number of birthdays? (M1)
- Show the children a selection of birthday cards that feature ages. Help them to put the cards in number order. Ask them to lay on each card cake candles, counters or beads to match the age. (M1)

Understanding the World

- Begin a group calendar of celebrations. Include events that are special to a specific child and, also, ones that are more widely known. Encourage children to bring in photos of themselves celebrating and to explain what they do and why it is special. (UW1)
- Look at examples (either real ones or pictures on the internet) of the red packets that are given to children to celebrate the Chinese New Year. Talk about what is inside. Explain that depending on the country where the celebration is taking place the coins and notes

inside will differ. Ask carers to lend coins from different countries and encourage children to compare the similarities and differences. Use black wax crayons and paper to make rubbings of the coins. (UW2, 3)

Expressive Arts and Design

- Sing the traditional 'happy birthday to you' song but replace children's names with claps or instrument beats. Can the children identify who the claps represent? Also enjoy adding new lines. (e.g. Happy birthday to us, Happy birthday to us, Happy birthday dear XX, Let's ride on a bus!) (EAD1)
- On postcard sized pieces of card make self portraits (whole body) for the 'birthday train'. (EAD1)

Activity: Egg games for Easter

Learning opportunity: Developing skills in aiming, throwing and catching.

Early Learning Goal: Physical Development. Moving and handling.

Resources: Balls to act as eggs, dessert spoons, a rope, children's names written on lolly sticks, plant pots, sand timer for a minute, plastic cones.

Key vocabulary: Easter, egg.

Organisation: Large group outside. Equipment set out in four defined areas for the activities below.

What to do: Talk to children about Easter eggs and the way that eggs are given at Easter to celebrate new life. Ask who has eaten an Easter egg. Then tell the children that in some parts of the world games, which use eggs, are played at Easter. These include throwing and catching eggs in France and egg rolling in countries such as America, Germany, Scotland and Switzerland.

Tell the children that the balls are pretend eggs. Introduce each activity area and explain what to do. Say that when the bell rings they need to stop what they are doing and move on to the next area. The activities are:

Throw an 'egg' – Children stand behind a rope and take it in turn to throw a ball, underarm as far as possible. Where the ball lands is marked with a named lolly stick. Each child is allowed several attempts with the stick marking their furthest throw.

Roll an egg – Balls are rolled as far as possible.

Egg and spoon – Children balance a ball on a spoon and see whether they can walk along a wavy, chalked line without dropping the 'egg'.

Aim an egg – The children stand in a hoop and aim their eggs to land in a plant pot (egg cup).

Finish by talking to the children about the activities. Which ones did they particularly enjoy? Which ones would they like to do again another day?

Activity: Counting with red money packets

Learning opportunity: Counting and solving problems with money.

Early Learning Goal: Mathematics. Numbers.

Resources: 6 red Chinese New Year money packets or red envelopes one containing five,1 pence coins, the others varying numbers of 1 pence coins; a 10 pence coin.

Key vocabulary: Chinese New Year, packet/envelope, coin, numbers to 20, more, fewest, greatest, smallest, red.

Organisation: Small group.

What to do: Show the children a red money packet. Explain that the colour red, for people from China, represents good luck, good wishes and happiness. Tell the children that the packets are given out at family gatherings to celebrate events such as the Chinese New Year and weddings.

Show the children the packet that contains five 1 pence coins. Together count the number of coins. How many are there? Ask a child to select one coin. What do they notice on the coin? Are there any numbers? Does anyone know its value?

Investigate the other packets. Ask which one contains the greatest number of coins? Which packet contains the fewest? Show the children the 10 pence and talk about its value. Do any of the packets equal 10 pence? Put the packets in pairs. How much money altogether is in each pair? Encourage the children to ask their own questions and solve problems.

Display

On separate pieces of A4 sized card print out, landscape, each month of the year. Cover a board with paper to represent blue sky and green grass and a black strip (ribbon, tape or border roll) as a railway track. Arrange the months as if carriages on a train. Add a red engine cut out from bright paper to the 'front' and round card circles for wheels.

On a second board begin a display of 'What we celebrate'. Talk to the children about what they would like to put on the board. Talk about the backing paper. What colours suggest 'celebration'? What types of events should the group add?

Theme 2: How we celebrate – special food and clothes

Communication and Language
- Look at wedding photos from around the world. Encourage the children to notice that there is wide variety in the clothes that are worn. (CL1)
- Share stories that feature celebrations and festivals. Look at the pictures to discover what the people wear and eat. (CL1)
- Look at photos of wedding bouquets and buttonholes. Give instructions for making flowers from circles of tissue paper. Make a group bouquet or buttonholes. (CL2)

Physical Development
- Look at pictures of people in Southern Ireland doing Irish dancing. Talk about the clothes they are wearing. Enjoy dancing to traditional Irish music. (PD1)
- Put out a range of clothes that might be worn for a celebration. Encourage children to explore the fastenings. How quickly can they get dressed? (PD1)

Personal, Social and Emotional Development
- Talk about harvest festivals, as times when thanks are given for both food and the people who grow and provide the foods. Make lists of people they would like to thank, and foods that the children particularly like. Use empty food packaging to make a group, harvest display. (PSE1, 3)
- Make a collection of sari fabrics. Talk about celebrations when saris might be worn. Provide strips of fabric for children to enjoy dressing dolls in saris and to role-play attending a celebration. (PSE1, 3)

Literacy
- Write menus for a celebration. (L2)
- Make a word collection of foods for celebrations. This might include latkes (for Hanukkah), sweet dates (for Eid) and mince pies (for Christmas). (L1, 2)
- Pick a favourite book character that enjoys eating such as Paddington Bear (marmalade) or the Hungry Caterpillar (many foods!). Share the story and then challenge the children to design a birthday cake for the character. Together write the recipe for the cake. (L1, 2)

Mathematics
- Print out some photos of tiered wedding cakes (e.g. from a royal wedding). Encourage children to count the layers. Use wooden bricks and cylinders or boxes to make models of wedding cakes. Which is the tallest cake? Which one could feed lots of people? How many? (M1, 2)
- Enjoy adding and subtracting with the rhyme 'Crown a cake with candles' (see activity opposite). (M1)
- Look at recipes of traditional foods made for celebrations such as Eid, Diwali and Rosh Hashanah. Explore the measurements within the recipes. Use a range of sizes of cups and spoons in the sand or water trays to role-play making celebratory foods. (M1, 2)

Understanding the World
- Use the internet to find pictures of henna patterns on hands. Talk about the celebrations for which hands might be decorated. Help children to make handprints and, when dry, decorate them with patterns drawn with black felt pens. (UW2, 3)

- Invite carers to donate special foods used at celebrations and ask them to explain the reasons for the foods. Having checked for food allergies, religious and diet preferences, enable children to enjoy taste testing. Record the session with photos. (UW2)

Expressive Arts and Design

- Look at photos of people going to weddings. Look at the range of transport used and the way some vehicles are decorated. Outside use wheeled toys, boxes and mime to enjoy going to a wedding. Provide ribbons and artificial flowers to decorate the toys and boxes. (EAD2)
- Make celebration necklaces (see activity right). (EAD1)
- Make models of celebration cakes from boxes. (EAD1)

Activity: Birthday cake number rhyme

Learning opportunity: Counting to 10. Solving number puzzles.

Early Learning Goal: Mathematics. Numbers

Resources: A photo of a birthday cake with candles.

Key vocabulary: Numbers to 10, candle, crowned, more, how many?

Organisation: Whole group.

What to do: Show the children the picture of the birthday cake with candles. Ask what it is. Talk about the way candles are used on birthday cakes to indicate the age of the birthday person. Together work out the age of the owner of the cake by counting the candles. Ask children how many candles they would need to crown their own, next birthday cake. Check children understand that 'crowning the cake' means putting on the candles.

Recite the 'Crown a cake with candles' number rhyme showing children the actions.

> **Crown a cake with candles number rhyme**
> To bake a cake is simple to do
> (*mime holding the bowl and mixing the cake*)
> But how many candles, I haven't a clue!
> (*hold hands out wide and shake the head*)
> Help me please!
> (*point to self on 'me'*)
> If I'm [10] today when just [8] can be found
> (*hold up 8 fingers*)
> How many more, for the cake to be crowned?
> (*hold up two more fingers*)
> Ruth Sutcliffe

Repeat the rhyme, encouraging children to join in with both the words and actions. Together solve the query by counting on from eight to ten. Repeat the rhyme with different ages and starting numbers of candles.

Activity: Designing and making celebration necklaces

Learning opportunity: Enjoying designing, cutting and decorating.

Early Learning Goal: Expressive Arts and Design. Exploring and using media and materials.

Resources: Large, white paper plates; examples of necklaces; photos of people wearing necklaces; scissors, felt pens, stickers, decorative materials requested by the children.

Key vocabulary: Celebration, jewelry, necklace.

Organisation: Small group.

What to do: Explain that when people enjoy dressing up for a celebration this also may include wearing special makeup and jewellery. Show the children examples of necklaces, and photos of people wearing necklaces. Encourage the children to pick out a necklace that they particularly like and to give reasons for their choice. Demonstrate how to cut out the rim of a paper plate and remove around 2cm from the 'necklace'.

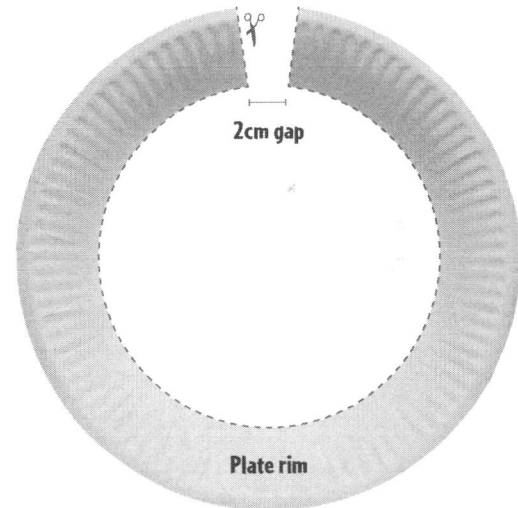

2cm gap

Plate rim

Place it around your neck. Show the children that it makes a good base for a necklace but that for a celebration it needs to be decorated. Encourage the children to name a celebration where their necklace might be worn and to make suggestions for the resources that they would like to use.

Display

Cover a board with bright, plain paper. Make a display label to say 'Necklaces for Celebrations'. Dependent on the number of necklaces to display, put up thread or wool lines over which the necklaces can hang. Display the necklaces along with a plastic mirror and a photo of the group wearing the necklaces.

Theme 3: How we celebrate – cards, lights and decorations

Communication and Language
- Show the children a range of cards for special occasions. Talk about the occasions that are being celebrated. Which ones have the children experienced? Ask children to select ones they particularly like and to explain why. (CL2)
- Look at the pictures on the cards. Invite children to tell stories about the pictures. Record the children talking and enjoy listening to their tales. (CL3)
- Help children to follow instructions to make paper flower decorations (see activity opposite). CL2

Physical Development
- Enjoy developing scissor skills by cutting up unwanted cards. Encourage the children to give reasons for the things they cut out and to use them in their play. (PD1)
- Outside enjoy being fireworks. Provide streamers and ribbons for the children to hold as they skip, run, twirl and jump in a large space. (PD1)
- Make divas, from clay, for Diwali. (PD1)

Personal, Social and Emotional Development
- Outside hide cards from celebrations and festivals for children to find. Give criteria for what they need to collect based on the location of the hiding place and the pictures on the cards. Invite children to hide cards and give clues for their hiding places. (PSE2)
- Make Rangoli patterns with sand or ground rice. Encourage the children to work in pairs and to select their own materials. When complete take photos. (PSE3

Literacy
- Make a group book where each page contains an envelope and card. As a group decide who is to receive the cards and why. Encourage children to write their own messages and to address the envelopes. The book might be to celebrate a book character's birthday or a non-fiction book on cards for celebrations around the world. (L2)
- Enjoy sharing the rhymes and words in birthday cards. Explore the words in cards from different religious festivals. (L1)

Mathematics
- Look at pictures of dragons from Chinese New Year celebrations. Make angry dragons from cardboard tubes, covered with red paper and linked with wool or treasury tags. Encourage children to use the word 'cylinder', to count the number of tubes used and to compare the lengths of the dragons. (M1, 2)

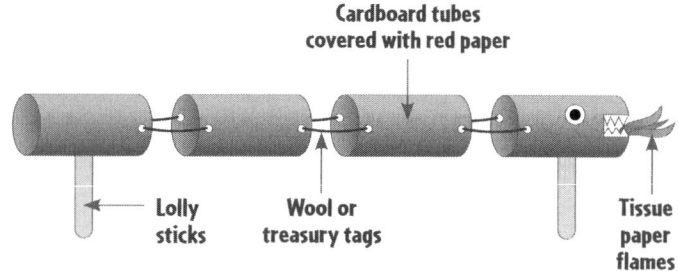

Cardboard tubes covered with red paper

Lolly sticks

Wool or treasury tags

Tissue paper flames

- Make paper chains. Count the paper loops in each chain. Which is the longest? Use the chains to measure large objects. (M1, 2)

Understanding the World
- Use technology to research Christingle decorations made from small oranges/satsumas, candles, ribbon and sweets/sultanas. Explain the orange is the world and the four cocktail sticks are for the seasons and also north, south, east and west. Discuss why and when they are given. Enjoy making Christingle decorations. (UW1, 3)

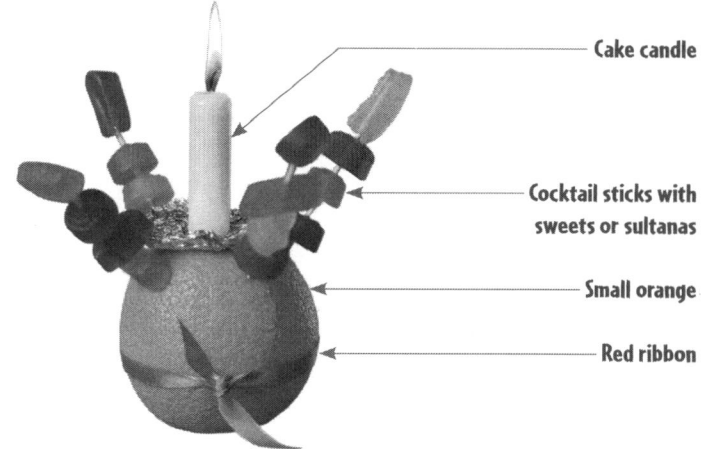

Cake candle

Cocktail sticks with sweets or sultanas

Small orange

Red ribbon

- Explain to the children how animals are used within the Chinese calendar to denote the year. Write the names on cards (Rat, Ox, Tiger, Rabbit, Dragon, Snake, Horse, Goat, Monkey, Rooster, Dog, Pig) and use these for sorting activities. Use the internet and books to find out interesting facts. (UW2, 3)
- Talk about firework displays and events they might celebrate. Make paper plate fireworks (see activity below). (UW1, 2, 3)

Expressive Arts and Design
- Use the cardboard tube dragons in dragon dances. (EAD2)
- Make songs based on decorations. (EAD1)
- Leave a range of shiny and sparkly materials for the children to invent their own decorations. Provide an area, inside or out for the children to decorate. Encourage them to use it in their role-play. (EAD1, 2)

Activity: Spiraling 'fireworks'

Learning opportunity: Talking and observing.

Early Learning Goal: Understanding the world. People and communities. The world. Technology.

Resources: White paper plates, sticky stars, hole punch, wool, iPad/tablet with access to the internet.

Key vocabulary: Firework, spiral.

Organisation: Small groups.

What to do: Talk to the children about firework displays. Discover whether they have seen fireworks before and the reasons for the displays. Watch appropriate firework displays on the internet. Which ones do the children like best? Can they explain why?

Demonstrate how to draw a spiral on a paper plate and cut along the line. Help children to draw their own spirals. When cut, decorate the spirals with shiny stars. Punch a hole at the centre and thread through it a piece of wool. Hold the centre and pull the edge to produce a snake like spiral.

Activity: Opening flower decorations

Learning opportunity: Listening to, and following, spoken instructions.

Early Learning Goal: Communication and Language. Understanding.

Resources: See the instructions sheet below.

Key vocabulary: Flower, petal, fold, open, close.

Organisation: Small group.
Print out in large font the following instructions.

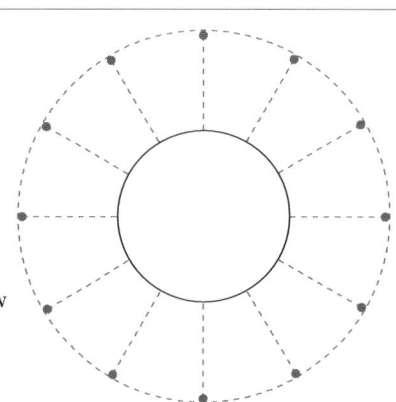

Opening flower decorations

What you will need
Scissors
Paper
Bowl of water
A large, round, plastic mug or similar to draw round
A round egg cup or similar to draw round

What you need to do
1. Draw around the mug.
2. Put the egg cup at the middle of the mug circle. Draw around the egg cup.
3. Think of a clock. Put a dot where the numbers go to show the hours. (It is easiest to this for 12, 3, 6 and 9 first and then put in the remaining dots.)
4. Snip from the dot to the inner circle to make the petals.
5. Fold the petals in turn towards the middle.
6. Float the flower on water and watch it open out.
7. Remove the flower and leave it to dry on a piece of paper towel. When dry it may be re-used.

What to do: Look at pictures of flower decorations used at celebrations and festivals. Encourage the children to notice the different types of flowers, their names, shapes and colours.

Talk about buds opening into flowers. Explain that today they are going to make paper flower decorations that will open if placed on a bowl of water.

Use the instructions sheet above to make paper daisies. When all the group have made a daisy, float them. Enjoy watching the flowers open. If the flowers are dried and re-used, in each successive go the daisy will open a little quicker.

Display

Hang the fireworks above a radiator. As hot air rises the 'fireworks' will spiral. On a board display the examples of celebration cards with a label that says 'Card shop for celebrations and festivals'. On a table in front, put a cash register, old cards and envelopes. Encourage children to role-play buying and selling cards. Also put out materials for the children to make new cards.

Theme 4: Celebrating diversity

Communication and Language
- Introduce the idea that everyone is different and special. Share picture books that feature children. Encourage the children to notice how the key characters differ and, also, the qualities that they share. (CL1, 2)
- Share stories that feature the celebration of festivals. Talk about the reasons for the celebrations and what the people, enjoying the festivals, do. (CL1, 2)
- Look at a globe or large, child-friendly world map. As a group begin to pick out familiar countries. Do the children know of special celebrations and festivals that happen in any countries? (CL1)

Physical Development
- Hold a 'Diversity Olympics' (see activity opposite). (PD1)
- Use chopsticks to transfer small, safe objects from one bowl to another. (PD1)
- Introduce the idea of a magic carpet which will take the children to different countries to find a celebration or festival. Explain that the carpet will take them to India. Enjoy dancing to traditional music. (PD1)

Personal, Social and Emotional Development
- Start to make 'All about me' boxes. Explain that each child will have a box and that it will include things that celebrate the child. This might be a special memory, a hand print, a fact about them or something they enjoy. Cover shoe boxes with wrapping paper chosen by the children. Help children to write their names on labels to identify their box. Send home a list of suggestions for things to include in the boxes (e.g. a photo of family, a favourite book, something from when they were younger). Use the boxes as a focus for discussion. Encourage the children to add things to the boxes over the weeks and to enjoy sharing them with their friends, their families and key adults in the setting. (PSE1, 2, 3)
- Make puppets from socks. Once made encourage children to notice the differences and similarities in their puppets. Encourage the children to enjoy using the puppets in both inside and outdoor play. Take the puppets for guided walks. (PSE1, 3)

Literacy
- Make name acrostics (see activity opposite). (L2)
- Show the children a dictionary. Ask the children to suggest words and together locate them. Begin a group dictionary of celebrations and festivals (e.g. **A**dvent, **B**irthday, **C**hristmas, **D**iwali, …) As the weeks progress encourage children and their families to think of more events to add to the group's celebrations dictionary. Explain that there may be more than one event for some letters whilst others may have none. (L1, 2)
- Talk about New Year celebrations (e.g. Seeing in the New Year and countdown to midnight, Chinese New Year, Rosh Hashanah). Talk about the New Year as a time to say goodbye to sad things, celebrate the past and look forward to the future. Enjoy writing New Year resolutions. These might be personal ones to go in the 'All About Me' boxes or for the group. (L2)

Mathematics
- Some celebrations and festivals happen at a time dependent on the phase of the moon. Use the internet to print out pictures showing the phases of the moon. Use everyday language to describe the shape and size of the moon. Provide yellow wax crayons and black paper to draw a night time scene with a moon. Again, encourage children to talk about the sizes and shapes of the moons. (M2)
- At the Jewish New Year (Rosh Hashanah), the shofar (a ram's horn) is sounded 100 times. Show the children a 100 square to give them a sense of the size of 100. Encourage children to enjoy counting to large numbers, inside and outside. (M1)

Understanding the World
- Invite carers to visit and talk about special celebrations and festivals. Encourage the children to ask questions. Use a tablet/iPad to record the visit. Later make a group book, using photos and use this to talk about the many different celebrations that happen. (UW1)
- Use the dictionary of celebrations and festivals (see Literacy) to make a list of ones that happen around the world (i.e. not the class birthdays). Look at a large calendar to try to find them. Remind the children that some celebrations and festivals happen on the same date each year but that others change. (UW2)
- One custom for the Chinese New Year is to make noise! Provide a range of resources for the children to make loud shakers. Investigate different containers such as cardboard boxes, plastic tubs and tins. Which resources make the loudest shaker? Can loud shakers be played quietly? What makes the loudest noise? (UW2)

Expressive Arts and Design

- Use long strips of paper (e.g. wall paper) to paint a whole group picture. Invite children to make handprints and footprints. Encourage them to notice the diverse range of sizes and shapes. Reinforce the notion that everyone is different, and everyone is special. (EAD1)

- Give children pages from magazines, newspapers and catalogues. Ask them to cut out faces and stick them on black squares (21cm by 21cm) of paper. When complete display them as a large collage of people. Look at the pictures. Encourage children to notice the range of appearances and facial expressions. Which people are happy? Which people have curly/long hair? (EAD1)

- Show the children examples of Rangoli patterns. Outside provide an area where children can chalk and enjoy making their own patterns. (EAD1)

Activity: Diversity Olympics

Learning opportunity: Enjoying physical challenges.

Early Learning Goal: Physical development. Moving and handling.

Resources: Photo or book showing Paralympic and Olympic events, paper planes, toy bricks, bubble mixture, wheeled toy and chalk, sand tray with hidden objects, water tray, skittles and ball, medal sized card circles with smiley faces threaded on to wool or ribbon (to be used as medals).

Key vocabulary: Olympics, Paralympics, events.

Organisation: Activity areas set out outside for children to access freely.

What to do: Show the children a book or pictures depicting Olympic and Paralympic events. Explain that there are teams, from many countries, and that people train hard in order to be selected to compete. Share pictures and reinforce that different people have different skills. Also show a picture of the medals that some people win.

Outside set challenges such as who can blow the largest bubble? Who can build the tallest tower? Who can find the hidden objects in the sand tray in the quickest time? Who can steer a wheeled toy along a wiggly line? Who can knock down nine skittles with one ball? Who can throw a paper plane the furthest? Who can spoon water quickly to fill a tub? Try to include a range of tasks, that develop both fine motor and gross motor skill. Over a week encourage the children to access a wide range of activities and to try to better their own performance. On the final day give all children medals made from card to celebrate competing.

Activity: My name acrostic

Learning opportunity: Enjoying looking for descriptive words.

Early Learning Goal: Literacy. Writing.

Resources: Paper, pencils, crayons, a book that reflects the diversity of people (e.g. 'Yoga Babies' by Fearne Cotton; 'Welcome to our world' by Moira Butterfield).

Key vocabulary: Acrostic, children's names, letter sounds

Organisation: Small group.

What to do: Share a book that reflects the diversity of people. Talk about the differences and the similarities. Reinforce that everyone is different and everyone is special.

Write vertically, on a large sheet of paper, the name of an adult in the setting in capital letters. Explain that together you are going to write an acrostic poem where each line starts with the letters in the name. Ask the children for suggestions of words that describe the person. For example, for Edmund:

Energetic
Daring
Messy
Understanding
Never late
Delightful

Help the children to make up acrostics for their own names. Compare acrostics and encourage the children to realise that differences can make them special! Later word-process the acrostics for a display and a group book. Encourage children to illustrate their own pages.

Display

Cover a table with cheerful, bright, celebratory wrapping paper or fabric. On the table put out a globe, and picture books which depict celebrations from around the world including key religious and cultural festivals.

Cover a small board with black paper and a cheerful border. Print out a title for the board: 'We all are different, we all are special!' Display some of the name acrostics on the board along with photos of the children. Place the remaining acrostics in plastic wallets and make a group book.

Theme 5: Music festivals around the world

Communication and Language

- Introduce the concept of a music festival. Explain that people who enjoy music come together to celebrate playing, singing and listening to music. Ask the children what type of music they would like to celebrate. Make a list of favourite songs. (CL1, 3)
- Explain that festivals of music take place around the world. Show photos from ones such as the annual Donauinselfest in Vienna, the Glastonbury Festival or Llangollen International Eisteddfod. Encourage the children to ask questions and to realise that going to a festival might require camping, eating food outside and even wellington boots! (CL1, 3)
- Use instruments from around the world to put sound effects to favourite stories. (CL1, 3)

Physical Development

- Enjoy dancing to music from around the world. (PD1)
- Use large equipment, rugs and boxes outside to role-play arriving at a music festival and setting up the camping area. (PD1)

Personal, Social and Emotional Development

- Listen to, and talk about, different types of music such as jazz, classical, folk, rock and roll … Ask the children what they think about the music. How do the pieces make them feel? Which pieces would be good at a music festival? Why? (PSE1, 3)
- Invite parents, who have attended a music festival, to come and talk about their experiences. Did they enjoy the festival? Was it very crowded? What was the music like? Encourage the children to ask questions. (PSE1)
- Talk about experiences of camping in tents. Encourage children who have spent nights in tents to share their experiences. (PSE1)

Literacy

- Design and make colourful posters to advertise a music festival. (L2)
- Set up a role-play ticket office, inside or outdoors. Provide a diary, telephone, card and pens to make tickets, sticky notes and a cash register. Encourage children to enjoy writing tickets, receipts and notes as they role-play selling and buying tickets for a music festival. (L1, 2)

Mathematics

- Enjoy number problems using drums, triangles or tuned percussion. Ask children to choose an instrument and play a given number of beats. Ask them to listen and count as you play an instrument. Challenge them to play their instrument the same number of times/one fewer/one more…(M1)
- Make panpipes from straws of varying lengths and corrugated card. Encourage children to compare straw lengths. Which is the shortest straw? Which is the longest (see activity opposite)? (M2)

Understanding the World

- Design sandwiches for a festival. Having checked for food allergies and religious and diet preferences, enjoy making and tasting the sandwiches. (UW2)
- Explore musical instruments from around the world. Investigate how the sounds are made. Enjoy making instruments for a festival. (UW2)
- Talk about the potential difficulties of finding a tent when thousands of people are camping at a music festival. Make flags, which could be attached to a tent. Discuss the need to make the flag stand out and to be waterproof. Provide a range of materials. When made, display the flags outside. (UW2)
- Use the internet to find photos of the 'biggest music festivals far and wide'. (UW3)

Expressive Arts and Design

- Set up a role-play tent area for the children to enjoy camping at a music festival. Encourage the children to make suggestions for the resources they would like to include. (EAD2)
- Set up an area with tuned and untuned percussion. Encourage the children to enjoy playing rhythms. Record the rhythms and use them for dancing. (EAD2)
- Use tuned percussion to make music based on the pentatonic scale (e.g. Using the notes C, D, E, G, A) (see activity opposite). (EAD2)

Activity: Making straw pipes for a music festival

Learning opportunity: Comparing lengths of straws and arranging them in size order.

Early Learning Goal: Mathematics. Shape, space and measures.

Resources: Scissors, corrugated card/plastic or tape; sample of panpipe music (see Youtube); panpipes or a picture of panpipes; plastic or paper straws (4 straws per child); sticky labels and a pencil.

Key vocabulary: Panpipes, numbers to five; longer, shorter, longest, shortest, the same.

Organisation: Small group.

What to do: Listen to a piece of panpipe music. Encourage the children to describe what they hear and to suggest the instrument(s) that play the music. Show a picture (or real panpipes) and explain that sounds are made by blowing across the tops of the pipes. Ask how the children think different sounds are made.

Show the children an example of straw pipes and explain how it can be made. Ask the children to cut a straw so that it is the same length as the longest one in the example straw pipes. Using the spare piece repeat for the next longest straw. Repeat this until each child has five pieces of straw of varied lengths. Ask them to arrange them in length order, longest to shortest. When cut, demonstrate how to place the pieces within the corrugated card/plastic. (If this is not available the straws may be taped onto a small rectangle of stiff card.) Once made give each child a label so that they may name their straw pipes.

Replay the panpipe music and encourage the children to enjoy blowing across their own instruments to add to the music. After playing, dry the pipes on a piece of paper towel and place them in the children's 'All about me boxes' (see Theme 4). This will ensure that children only play the pipes that they have made!

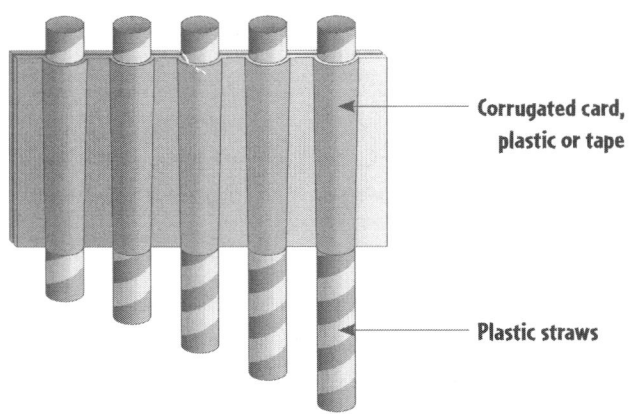

Corrugated card, plastic or tape

Plastic straws

Activity: Composing music for a festival

Learning opportunity: Playing tuned and untuned percussion instruments, composing, listening and collaborating.

Early Learning Goal: Expressive Arts and Design. Exploring and using media and materials.

Resources: Chime bars for the notes C, D, E, G and A; tambourines, bells and shakers; examples of music that might be played at a parade to celebrate the Chinese New Year; equipment to record the music.

Key vocabulary: Names of the instruments used, quiet, loud, repeat, again, Chinese New Year.

Organisation: Small group of up to four children in an area where other children will not be disturbed!

What to do: Listen to a joyful piece of Chinese music such as music that might be played at a parade to celebrate the Chinese New Year (look on Youtube). Encourage the children to listen for the types of instruments that are played and for repeating notes. Explain that at music festivals people enjoy listening to favourite pieces of music and, also, brand new compositions. Say that today you are going to help them make a new piece of music.

Show the children the chime bars. Look for the note letter on each one and play the note. Compare the sounds. Invite a child to play CCDDCCD CCDDCCD whilst at the same time you play the notes EGEGAAA EGEGAAA. (The joy of a pentatonic scale is that the five notes can be played in any combination and will always sound good.) Ask a second child to select a piece of untuned percussion and to provide a steady beat as the chime bars are played. Finally ask a third child to take over your chime bars. (Further percussion can be added if more than three children are participating.) Repeat the composition several times and, when everyone is content, record the piece. Listen to the piece. Could it be improved? How? Continue enjoying the composing of music, ensuring that children share the instruments and all get a chance to use the chime bars.

Over the coming days repeat the activity with other children and, also, allow children to use the instruments for child-initiated activity. When all children have been recorded combine the pieces for use at the parade of party clothes during the final Celebration Party (see page 20).

Display
Cover a display board with dark blue or black paper to be a night sky and the lower half green for grass. Cut out shapes to resemble tents. Display the children's tent flags on the tents. On a table set out instruments from around the world along with the chime bars and other percussion instruments.

Theme 6: A special party

Communication and Language

- Introduce the idea of a special, celebration party. Ask the children to make suggestions for the reasons they might hold the party. Talk about the kinds of things that might happen and emphasise that the party will be a time for sharing. (CL2, 3)
- Share stories about parties. How did the characters celebrate? What did they wear? What did they eat? (CL1)
- Tell children that the party will celebrate 'our world'. Share books that encourage children to notice the similarities and differences in people throughout the world. (CL1)

Physical Development

- Enjoy traditional party games that involve movement such as 'Simon says', 'musical statues' and 'follow my leader'. (PD1)
- Tell a story about going to a party. Begin by saying 'We're going to a party'. Repeat the phrase throughout the story. Encourage the children to move and mime to the words. Also encourage the children for suggestions of lines. (PD1)
- Use play dough to create birthday teas for characters in books. (PD1)

Personal, Social and Emotional Development

- Talk about manners for a party. Discuss the need to say please and thank you. (PSE2)
- Talk about hopes and dreams. Write fortunes for 'Our World party fortune cookies' (see Bringing it All Together). Write the 'fortunes' on pieces of clean greaseproof paper. (PSE1, 3)
- Make 'party messy mats' (see activity opposite). (PSE1)

Literacy

- Begin to make a group big book to record the preparation for the party and the actual party. (L2)
- Show the children a cracker. Explore the contents and share the joke. Enjoy writing cracker jokes. (L1, 2)
- Make menus for a party tea. (L2)

Mathematics

- Play party games which involve counting, giving directions and shape. Examples include:
  - Pass the parcel using dice to decide how many times the parcel is passed on. (M1)
  - Musical shapes. Put out a range of paper shapes (e.g. square, triangle, circle, oblong, diamond, star … Children dance to music. When it stops they stand near a shape. The name of one shape is then called out and all standing near the shape gain a sticky star or dot. (M2)
  - Pin the tail on the donkey (or could be related to a theme – pin the nose on Father Christmas …). Children work as a group where one child wears a blindfold and the rest of the group give directions so that the tail is pinned accurately. (M2)
  - Skittles. (M1)
- Make wrapping paper with repeating patterns by printing with solid shapes. Encourage the children to name the shapes that they select and to describe their patterns. (M2)

Understanding the World

- Talk about the custom of giving out party bags at the end of a birthday party. Has anyone ever been given a party bag? What was in it? Examine a collection of party bags. From which materials are they made? Which bag is the prettiest? Which one is the strongest? Do the bags have handles? How are they made? Which bag would hold the most? Provide materials for the children to enjoy making their own party bags. (UW1, 2)
- Use the internet and conversations with carers to research party food from around the world. (UW3)
- Enjoy making crackers that do not bang (see activity opposite). (UW2)

Expressive Arts and Design

- Make party crowns, from strips of card decorated with thumbprints, sequins and stars. (EAD1)
- To the tune of 'Twinkle, twinkle, little star' write a party song. This might include complete lines or simply a list of party words. For example:

  Party, party, party time
  Invitations, party time!
  Crackers, food and games to play,
  Pretty clothes and fun today,
  Party, party, party time
  Invitations, party time!

  Encourage the children to make up actions and add percussion. Record the songs for later use. (EAD1)

Activity: Making party messy mats

Learning opportunity: Sharing and selecting resources.

Early Learning Goal: Personal, Social and Emotional Development. Self-confidence and self-awareness.

Resources: Examples of placemats; A4 paper in a variety of colours; wrapping paper with distinct shapes; glue-sticks; wax-crayons, scissors, laminating pouches and a laminator.

Key vocabulary: Words to describe the resources and wrapping paper pictures/shapes.

Organisation: Small group.

What to do: Explain that some people like to use placemats when they eat a meal. Look at examples of placemats and encourage the children to think of times when they might be useful. Explain that at the party picnic tea it would be useful to have named mats that can show them where to sit and, also, be helpful for stopping mess get on the floor.

Show the children the available resources. Ask them to write their name in the centre of their mat and then cut out from the wrapping paper things to decorate their mat. Encourage the children to plan before sticking and to share resources. Wax crayons can be used in spare space. Dots in different colours will create a happy, party time effect. Tell the children their 'messy mats' will be laminated and ask why the laminating is a good idea.

Once made the mats may be saved for the party.

Activity: Making crackers which do not bang!

Learning opportunity: Comparing similarities and differences in papers. Making crackers.

Early Learning Goal: Understanding the World. The world.

Resources: Two examples of crackers; jokes printed on small slips of paper; cardboard tubes cut to cracker size; range of papers (e.g. tissue, crepe, magazine, newsprint); glue, tape, scissors, small toys, thread/wool/present ribbon.

Key vocabulary: Names of materials; cracker, joke, bang.

Organisation: Whole group introduction; small group for the practical activity.

What to do: Show the children the crackers. What is on the crackers? When might they be used? Talk about the paper which the crackers use and encourage the children to realise that it needs to tear easily when pulled. Rattle the crackers and invite suggestions for what might be inside.

Pull a cracker, ensuring it is not near a child's face, and examine the contents. What do the children think about what is inside? Is there a hat? Does it fit? Is the joke funny? Did the children like the bang? Explain that some people do not like bangs and that the group is going to make crackers for the party which do not bang.

Small group cracker making: Invite children to select the materials they wish to use to make their cracker. Encourage them to give reasons for their paper choice. Invite them to select a joke and a toy to go inside the cracker. Demonstrate how three tubes may be laid end to end, such that when the chosen paper is rolled around the tubes a thread may be tied in the gaps between the tubes. This helps the central tube not to move and results in a symmetrical cracker. Finish by decorating the cracker with stickers and felt pen patterns. When complete, name the crackers and keep them safe to take home at the end of the party.

Display

Near a role-play kitchen, the sand tray or water tray, display the menus on a board or in plastic wallets in a book. Encourage the children to enjoy using the menus in their role-play.

Bringing it all together

Holding a group party will let the children experience the pleasure that can come from making plans and preparations which result in a successful, fun occasion. Plans for the party might include making suggestions for the games, food, invitations/cards, and the guest list.

The Celebration Party

Theme
There are many possible themes for the 'Celebration Party' including: Christmas, Easter, Diwali, Chinese New Year; End of term; a national event … Some groups may like to choose a theme with the children. Others may decide to use a theme such as 'Our world' where a number of festivals and celebrations may be included dependent on the actual children in the setting. All parties though are likely to share the key elements of dressing up, food, presents, decorations, games, and sharing.

Food
- Use biscuit cutters to make shaped sandwiches such as stars, hearts and gifts to fit the party theme.
- Make fruit kebabs. Ask the children to make suggestions for their favourite fruits. Talk about the countries where the fruits were grown.
- Make cookies using ingredients which cater for any food allergies, religious and diet preferences. When made, lay the cookies on the fortunes, written by the children on greaseproof paper, folded into four.
- Make party drinks by combining a range of fruit juices with sparkling water. Again, talk about the countries where the fruits have been grown.
- Make ice cubes with fruit juice in trays with shapes to fit the party theme.
- Make picnic table cloths for the party tea by giving groups of children large sheets of paper to decorate with wax crayon patterns and pictures. (Do not use felt pens as ink will run if the cloths get wet.)

Gifts
- In a week prior to the party ask carers to donate unwanted children's toys and books. Give each child a label with a peer's name. Tell them that this is the person to whom they will give a present. Invite them to select a gift ensuring they know it is what they are giving. Encourage them to think about their peer and what they think they would like. Use the wrapping paper made during the Special Party theme, to wrap the parcels. Remember to stick on the label. Place the wrapped parcels in a large sack. Remind the children of festivals and celebrations where people enjoy giving and receiving gifts. Also talk about the need to keep what is in the gift a secret!

Clothes
- In the weeks prior to the party ask carers to donate unwanted, clean T-shirts (plain ones if possible). Explain that the shirts will be worn at the party. Provide fabric pens or crayons for the children to enjoy decorating the shirts. (Remember to write the child's name on their shirt label.)

Games
- With children make a list of favourite party games, played over the course of the Celebrations and Festivals themed weeks, which they would like to replay at the party. Make a pass the parcel with stickers in each layer and spare ones for any child who does not open a paper layer. Ask for suggestions of other games and encourage the children to explain how they are run. Also, prepare games which may be new to children. When planning the order for games ensure there is a balance of ones that involve movement and those which require sitting.

The party
Begin the party with a clothes parade of children wearing their party T-shirts. Play the music composed by the children (see Theme 5: Expressive Arts and Design). Some children may also like to wear the paper plate necklaces made during Theme 3. Take a group photo and, also, further photos throughout the party to add to the 'party big book' (see Theme 6 Literacy).

When introducing games remind children of how they link to the Celebrations and Festivals themes. Try to encourage children to share and to support their peers.

Enjoy a picnic tea with children sitting, on the floor, around the paper cloths, with the messy mats to show where they sit. Ideally each group will have an adult to oversee the sharing of food and the serving of the drinks.

Invite collecting adults on the party day to arrive a little early so that they may join their children for the final part. Finish the party with a favourite story and songs enjoyed over the previous weeks. Finally exchange the gifts, wrapped by the children. Encourage them to say thank you! When the children go home, give out the crackers that the children made (see Theme 6: Understanding the World).

Resources

Resources to collect

- Used envelopes and red envelopes
- Used celebration cards
- Wrapping paper for a range of celebrations and festivals.
- Old calendars
- Items for role play (e.g. party clothes, resources for a role-play kitchen and music festival ticket office, a child-friendly tent)
- Crackers
- Method for taking photos and recording music
- Examples of artefacts, photos/pictures and clothes relevant to a range of celebrations and festivals.
- Examples of party bags
- Musical instruments from around the world including panpipes
- Chime bars (C, D, E, G, A), and a range of percussion instruments
- Chopsticks
- Red money packets given to celebrate the Chinese New Year
- 1 pence and 2 pence coins and examples of coins from around the world

Everyday resources

- Papers and cards of different weights; colours and textures available e.g. sugar paper, shiny papers
- Dry powder paints for mixing and mixed paints
- Different sized paintbrushes and paint mixing containers
- A variety of drawing and colouring pencils, crayons, pastels, felt pens etc.
- Additional decorative and finishing materials such as sequins, tinsel, shiny wool and threads, parcel ribbon
- Table covers
- Painting aprons
- String and wool
- Corrugated card
- Straws
- Tape
- Hole punch and stapler
- PVA glue
- Modelling dough and clay
- Sand and water trays with cups, spoons, bowls and plates
- Clean recyclable packaging (e.g. cereal packets, yogurt pots, cardboard tubes, bottle tops)

Books for children

- *The Jolly Christmas Postman* by Allan Ahlberg and Janet Ahlberg
- *The Queen's Knickers* by Nicholas Allan
- *Welcome to our world* by Moira Butterfield
- *Happy Birthday Blue Kangaroo* by Emma Chichester Clark
- *Yoga Babies* by Fearne Cotton
- *Katie Morag and the Wedding* by Mairi Hedderwick
- *Alfie and the Birthday Surprise* by Shirley Hughes
- *Kipper's Birthday* by Mick Inkpen
- *My First Ramadan* by Karen Katz
- *When Willie Went to the Wedding* by Judith Kerr
- *Elmer* by David McKee
- *My First Kids Jokes Ages 3-5* by Cindy Merrylove
- *Peppa's Christmas Post* by Peppa Pig
- *Peppa's Diwali* by Peppa Pig
- *Hassan and Aneesa Celebrate Eid* by Yasmeen Rahim
- *Happy Birthday Winnie* by Valerie Thomas and Korky Paul
- *My Very First Joke Book* by Kaye Umansky
- *My world, your world* by Melanie Walsh
- *Harry and the Dinosaurs have a Happy Birthday* by Ian Whybrow
- *Apples and Honey – A Rosh Hashannah Story* by Jonny Zucker
- *Eight Candle to Light – A Chanukah Story* by Jonny Zucker
- *Eight Dates to Eat – A Ramadan and Eid Story* by Jonny Zucker
- *It's Party Time – A Purim Story* by Jonny Zucker

Non-fiction picture books on a variety of celebrations.

Resources for planning

For additional ideas on festivals and celebrations see the following titles within the *Planning for Learning Through* series:

- *Autumn* (Harvest)
- *Food* (Food for special occasions)
- *Games* (Party games)
- *Spring* (Spring Parade)
- *The Twelve Days of Christmas*

For curriculum guidance use the internet to search for the national framework most relevant to your setting. For example, for settings in England, this would be:

- **England:** Department for Education (2014) 'Statutory Framework for the Early Years Foundation Stage' (http:// www.foundationyears.org.uk/eyfs-statutory-framework/)

Collecting evidence of children's learning

Monitoring children's development is an important task. Keeping a record of children's achievements will help you to see progress and will draw attention to those who are having difficulties for some reason. If a child needs additional professional help, such as speech therapy, your records will provide valuable evidence.

Profiles should cover all the areas of learning, as defined by the relevant UK framework and be the result of collaboration between practitioners, parents and carers. Parents should be made aware of your record keeping policies when their child joins your group. Show parents the types of documentation that you are keeping and make sure they understand their purpose. As a general rule, documentation should be open. Families should have access to their child's documentation at any time and know that they can contribute to it. Take regular opportunities to talk to parents about children's progress. If you have formal discussions regarding children about whom you have particular concerns, a dated record of the main points should be kept.

Keeping it manageable

Documentation should be helpful in informing practitioners, adult helpers and parents and always be for the benefit of the child. The golden rule is to keep it simple, manageable and useful. Do not try to make records following every activity!

Documentation will basically fall into two categories – observations and reflections:

Observations

- **Spontaneous observations:** Sometimes you will want to make a note of observations as they happen e.g. a child is heard counting cars accurately during a play activity, or is seen to play collaboratively for the first time.

- **Planned observations:** Sometimes you will plan to make observations of children's developing skills in their everyday activities. Using the learning opportunity identified for an activity will help you to make appropriate judgments about children's capabilities and to record them systematically.

To collect information:

- Talk to children about their activities and listen to their responses.
- Listen to children talking to each other.
- Observe children's work such as early writing, drawings, paintings and models. (Keeping photocopies or photographs can be useful in tracking progress. Photographs are particularly useful to monitor children's development in the outdoor environment.)

Sometimes it may be appropriate to set up 'one off' activities for the purposes of monitoring development. Some groups, for example, ask children to make a drawing of themselves to record their progressing skills in both co-ordination and observation. Do not attempt to make records following every activity!

Reflections

It is useful to spend regular time reflecting on the children's progress. Aim to make some brief comments about each week and discuss these regularly with colleagues and families.

Informing your planning

Collecting evidence about children's progress is time consuming and it is important that it is useful. When you are planning, use the information you have collected to help you to decide what learning opportunities you need to provide next for children. For example, a child who has poor pencil or brush control will benefit from more play with dough or construction toys to build the strength of hand muscles.

Example observation sheet

Name: Lucy Green

Date: 31.1.20

Area of Learning: Mathematics. Count reliably with numbers from 1 to 20.

Context (Please tick):

Child-initiated: √   **Adult-led:**

Alone: **In a group:** √

Observation: Lucy is playing outside with two friends. She is trying to build the tallest tower and counting the bricks. "1, 2, 3, 4, 5, 7, 8. Mine's 8. Yours is only 7." She knocks the tower down, chuckles and starts to build again, counting as she places the bricks. "1, 2, 3, 4, 5, 7." The tower falls over. "Oops. I wanted to do 20."

What next: Check Lucy knows 6 follows 5. Encourage use of the outdoor counting grids, skittles and number rhyme CD.

Observer: R. Gillham

Overview of areas covered through 'Celebrations and Festivals'

Theme	Communication and Language	Physical Development	Personal, Social and Emotional Development	Literacy	Mathematics	Understanding the World	Expressive Arts and Design
What we celebrate	Listening and attention Understanding Speaking	Moving and handling Health and self-care	Self-confidence and self-awareness Managing feelings and behaviour Making relationships	Reading Writing	Numbers Shape, space and measures	People and communities The world Technology	Exploring and using media and materials Being imaginative
How we celebrate – special food and clothes	Listening and attention Understanding Speaking	Moving and handling Health and self-care	Self-confidence and self-awareness Managing feelings and behaviour Making relationships	Reading Writing	Numbers Shape, space and measures	People and communities The world Technology	Exploring and using media and materials Being imaginative
How we celebrate – cards, lights and decorations	Listening and attention Understanding Speaking	Moving and handling Health and self-care	Self-confidence and self-awareness Managing feelings and behaviour Making relationships	Reading Writing	Numbers Shape, space and measures	People and communities The world Technology	Exploring and using media and materials Being imaginative
Celebrating diversity	Listening and attention Understanding Speaking	Moving and handling Health and self-care	Self-confidence and self-awareness Managing feelings and behaviour Making relationships	Reading Writing	Numbers Shape, space and measures	People and communities The world Technology	Exploring and using media and materials Being imaginative
Music festivals around the world	Listening and attention Understanding Speaking	Moving and handling Health and self-care	Self-confidence and self-awareness Managing feelings and behaviour Making relationships	Reading Writing	Numbers Shape, space and measures	People and communities The world Technology	Exploring and using media and materials Being imaginative
A special party	Listening and attention Understanding Speaking	Moving and handling Health and self-care	Self-confidence and self-awareness Managing feelings and behaviour Making relationships	Reading Writing	Numbers Shape, space and measures	People and communities The world Technology	Exploring and using media and materials Being imaginative

Note: For each theme, highlight the Early Learning Goal areas covered, through both adult focused and child-initiated activities, relating to 'Celebrations and Festivals'.

Home links

The theme of Celebrations and Festivals lends itself to useful links with children's homes and families. Through working together children and adults gain respect for each other and build comfortable and confident relationships.

Establishing partnerships

- Keep parents informed about the themes for Celebrations and Festivals and the activities that children will experience. By understanding the work of the group, parents will enjoy the involvement of contributing ideas, time and resources.
- Photocopy the 'family page' for each child to take home.
- Ask for volunteers to assist with the Celebration Party picnic.
- Invite the adults, who collect the children from the Celebration Party, to arrive a little early so they may share in a story, singing and the exchange of party gifts.

Visiting enthusiasts

- Invite adults to come to the group to talk about family celebrations and festivals.
- Investigate whether there are any adults who have skills or knowledge they might share with the children such

as experience of icing and decorating celebration cakes; taking photographs at parties and weddings; camping at a music festival and making decorations.

Resource requests

- Ask parents to contribute greetings cards, old calendars and interesting papers and materials that could be used for making decorations.
- Ask parents to donate plain T-shirts to decorate as party clothes, and unwanted toys/books to wrap as party presents. Also, collect small toys suitable to go in crackers.
- Ask for items which might be borrowed for a display on festivals and celebrations. If items are too precious to lend ask whether photos of them could be taken and copied in the setting.
- Tell parents about the 'All about me boxes' that will be introduced during the 'Celebrating Diversity' theme. Invite them to help their children select/make items to include in the boxes.

The special party

- It is always useful to have extra adults at parties. Involve them in overseeing games and in helping to set out the picnic tea.
- Invite parents to make suggestions of party games. Seek help in games which require preparation such as:
  - The card game where cards are cut into puzzles with 6 pieces. Children are put into pairs and given one piece of a puzzle. The other pieces are placed around the room. Children then search for their missing pieces and then make the puzzles.
  - Pin the nose on Santa.
  - Find the pair where each child is given a red envelope containing four cloakroom tickets. The matching numbers are then hidden around the room (or outside) for children to find in the quickest, possible time.
  - The making game where children are given identical objects and challenged to make a gift. Objects might include clean yogurt pots, cardboard tubes, cotton reels, lolly-sticks, tape...